Q&A Freud

...off The Record

D.M. Thomas

Foreword By Edward De Bono

16

EasyRead Large

RHYW

Copyright Page from the Original Book

Freud
D.M. Thomas

This edition first published in the United Kingdom and Ireland in 2010
by Watkins Publishing, an imprint of Duncan Baird Publishers Ltd
Sixth Floor, Castle House
75–76 Wells Street, London W1T 3QH

Conceived, created and designed by Duncan Baird Publishers

Managing Editors: Peggy Vance and Gill Paul
Co-ordinating Editor: James Hodgson
Editor: Kirty Topiwala
Managing Designer: Clare Thorpe

British Library Cataloguing-in-Publication Data:
A CIP record for this book is available from the British Library

ISBN: 978-1-907486-62-3
10 9 8 7 6 5 4 3 2 1
Typeset in Dante MT and Baskerville BT
Printed in Shanghai by Imago

Publisher's note:
The interviews in this book are purely fictional, while having a solid basis in biographical fact. They take place between a fictionalized Sigmund Freud and the author, D.M. Thomas. This literary work has not been approved or endorsed by the Freud estate.

TABLE OF CONTENTS

FOREWORD by Edward de Bono

The human brain craves explanations. That is why very young children are always asking "why?" Explanations tie things together. They explain why things happen and also allow us to predict future behaviour.

Throughout history, people have searched for such explanations in order to make sense of their lives. First there was magic and religion to explain how things were organized, then there was science and its disengaged laws, and somewhere in between these two was Freud. Just as Voltaire said of God, if Freud had not existed it would have been necessary to invent him.

Freud's whole edifice was a masterwork of explanation, with sex at its core. He studied his own, often depressed, mind as well as those of his patients, accounting for our actions and troubled thoughts with revolutionary theories such as infant sexuality, sublimation, the symbolism of dreams and the Oedipus complex. He believed that if something was not as visible in a patient's personality as it should have been, that was because it was too painful and had to be repressed. A strange symptom, such as a nervous tic or a cough, might really be a displacement for the memory of a far more taboo experience or emotion. "Hysterics suffer mainly from reminiscences," as he and Joseph Breuer famously concluded.

These theories shocked, troubled and intrigued people, and ensured Freud a central role in psychology. Were they true in the scientific sense? Possibly, in some cases. Perhaps not in others. Before the sex hormones sensitize various nerve pathways at puberty, it is hard to see how sex could operate in infants and children. It might have been more accurate to talk of "pleasure" and "love" rather than sex – however, that would only have weakened Freud's explanations. The "truth" in his work is not really what matters. It was as much poetry as science: his theories created stories that people could believe in. These stories had a real value in allowing a patient to "understand" his or her behaviour or symptoms, and as a result of such understanding things often did get better.

Like it or not, Freud remains an inescapable influence on the way we think about ourselves, and each other, today. We should consider him the master explainer, a phenomenon placed somewhere between poetry and science, and between psychology and magic.

INTRODUCTION

I am often asked, "Why Freud? Why are you so fascinated by him?" The fascination is certainly there; in two of my novels, *The White Hotel* and *Eating Pavlova,* he is a major character and narrator. How could I resist an invitation to have meetings with him in the timeless unconscious, at a splendid café where one can still smoke?

Often reviled as a sex-crazed fantasist when he founded psychoanalysis, he is attacked by many once again, a century later. He is accused of intellectual dishonesty, undervaluing women, and overvaluing both his theories and the effectiveness of psychoanalysis. Even if his ideas had some validity in the patriarchal bourgeois Vienna of 1900, critics say, they don't apply in our fluid, multicultural, post-feminist society.

There is a grain of truth in all these criticisms except that of intellectual dishonesty. We all sometimes deceive ourselves – Freud less than most – but being truthful was his greatest pride. In his maturity, he saw psychoanalysis as ministering to the soul (Psyche), man's whole essence, not just his mind. Fascinated by archaeology, he was an archaeologist of the unconscious, whom we ignore at our peril.

The psyche as Freud saw it was profoundly poetry-making, constantly creating by metaphor and symbol; and that strikes me as both true and inspiring

– unlike our age's model of the mind as a computer. Freud's "eternal Eros" has been tamed by sexologists and mechanistic porn, and infantilized by sex toys and talk of "blow jobs". Many who are hostile to him are repressing uncomfortable truths about themselves, preferring to seek answers to problems in sociology or politics. Freud faced his own demons, fearlessly, and wished us to face ours.

Even if his model of the psyche should prove to be more of a rich poetic metaphor than scientifically accurate, it will not lessen his greatness. He is more illuminating when wrong than others when they are right, for he has the wisdom of the ages to call on. He drew inspiration from ancient myths; and loved the great writers, such as Shakespeare and Dostoyevsky, who he said had discovered the unconscious before him. Despotic at times, he was nevertheless a liberator. Diana Hume George, author of *Blake & Freud,* quotes, "No individual can keep these Laws, for they are death/to every energy of man," and asks whether, but for the line-break, any scholar would know this was William Blake writing, not Freud. They both wanted to free men and women from their chains, their "mind-forged manacles". Though conservative in his views on "women's rights", he gave dignity to women by treating them as sexual beings.

Voyaging alone deep into the human psyche, in his most excited, creative spells Freud knew he was "not at all a scientist, not an observer, not an experimenter, not a thinker. I am by temperament nothing but a conquistador – an adventurer." This is the Freud I love.

SIGMUND FREUD (1856–1939)

His Life in Short

Jacob Freud, Sigmund's father, first emerges dimly in the 1840s as an archetypal Wandering Jew, from Galicia (now split between Poland and Ukraine), the most easterly, primitive and anti-Semitic part of the sprawling, polyglot Hapsburg empire. With his maternal grandfather, he drove a horse and cart the hundreds of miles between east and west, trading wool and honey for dyed cloth. He had a wife called Sally, who before he was eighteen had borne him two sons, Emanuel and Philipp. Eventually, when approaching 40, Jacob moved west to the town of Freiberg (now Příbor in the Czech Republic); and in 1855 – described as a widower, with the deceased wife named, mysteriously, not Sally but Rebekka – he remarried. "Rebekka" remains unexplained. His new wife, Amalie, was just nineteen, attractive and feisty, a Galician Jewess who had been living with her family in Vienna. Within a year, on 6 May 1856, she gave birth to her "golden Sigi" – at about the time that Emanuel and his wife were giving Jacob his first grandchild.

It may have felt a trifle odd to the unmarried Philipp to be greeting a pretty stepmother his own age. Some have even suggested, from an imaginative reading of one of Freud's dreams, that Amalie and Philipp may have become rather too close; and that this may be why Jacob's two older sons left home to settle in England. In any event, the unusual family grouping was fruitful soil for the future discoverer of the Oedipus complex.

Amalie bore a second son, who quickly died; then five daughters and finally a son who survived. When Sigmund was four, Jacob moved his family to the great imperial capital, Vienna. It is not known how Jacob earned his living: money was certainly tight. Thousands of other less fortunate Jews were streaming into Vienna from *shtetls* in the east, to eke out a living as pedlars. They seemed – even to middle-class Jews like the Freuds – an alien presence, inevitably encouraging anti-Semitism.

A brilliant pupil at a state high school, his German fluent and stylish, Sigmund was on his way to casting off religious and cultural Jewishness. He learned several languages including Greek and Latin. He first read Shakespeare at eight. There was no question which child counted the most in the Freud household: one of the girls asked for and was given a piano, but when Sigmund complained that the noise made it impossible to study, the piano went.

For someone who would become obsessionally focused once he had found life's purpose, Freud moved toward it uncertainly and slowly. At first he thought of becoming a lawyer; then determined on a career as a natural scientist. He enrolled in the medical department of the University of Vienna in 1873, with more interest in zoological research than in practising medicine. He examined nerve cells in the spinal cords of fish, sought to discover if male eels possessed testicles. He meandered, endlessly curious, not bothering to graduate till 1882. This was also the year when he fell in love with a German Jewish girl living in Vienna, Martha Bernays.

Sweet and compliant, she was living quietly with her widowed mother. Too soon, for Freud, they moved back to their native Hamburg. Martha had other admirers; Freud was jealous; and while he endlessly praised her sweetness, when her letters seemed too tame he confessed to her, "I can hardly contain myself for silent savagery." His letters are romantic rather than erotic, however: the furthest he went was to recall a country walk in which she had turned aside to pull up her stockings. Realizing he would need more than his tiny research salary for marriage, he spent three years at the Vienna General Hospital, preparing to practise medicine. His heart was not in it – he feared, as he told a friend, mediocrity – but he buckled down.

He experimented with cocaine, seeing it for a while as a wonder-drug, boosting vitality. He may have slept with a prostitute in Paris, where in 1885–6 he spent several months at the Salpêtrière Hospital, under the famous neurologist Charcot: most Viennese doctors had their first sex with "lower-class" girls – but essentially Freud waited for Martha and marriage.

These largely lonely months, with Charcot as guide, provided the vital clue to his future. He would specialize, not in organic illnesses, but in neuroses – illness created by the mind.

A large framed photograph in Freud's consulting room at 19 Berggasse, where he would spend most of his married life, shows a bosomy, corseted woman swooning in the arms of an assistant – possibly Freud himself – while Charcot demonstrates his therapeutic technique to a hallful of men. A classic pre-feminist picture. Charcot showed that many physical symptoms, such as paralyses, bore no relation to physiology but only to the patient's imagined concept of how her body worked. "Her" because this condition, hysteria (from the Greek word for "womb"), was most often seen in women. Charcot used hypnotism to induce his patients to reveal hysterical effects. A word would make her go into convulsions, or fall screaming to the floor. Freud was convinced: he was drawn to theatricality and, as the photograph suggested, there was an aura of sex which must have appealed to him too.

He married Martha in Hamburg in 1886, took her to Vienna and rented a four-roomed flat. There he treated patients suffering from nervous complaints. He used hypnosis, like Charcot, but increasingly also the technique of "free association" – letting patients follow the trail of their own thoughts, while lying on his couch. An older friend, the physician Joseph Breuer, helped by sometimes sending him patients.

Freud's choice of specialism chimed in with the mood of *fin de siècle* Vienna. Richard Krafft-Ebing published his ground-breaking study of morbid sexuality, *Psychopathia Sexualis,* in 1886. At the very top of the faltering empire, the Emperor Franz Joseph was obsessional, the Empress Elisabeth half-mad. In 1889 the Crown Prince, Rudolf, shot himself and his mistress, in what was probably a double suicide, after one last act of love: a vivid embodiment of the prevailing fascination with sex and death.

In 1895, Freud and Breuer jointly published *Studies in Hysteria.* Unlike his rather prim mentor, Freud was sure that the hysterical symptoms he observed in patients were sexual in origin, that the body created a diversionary illness to block off unruly desires and memories which would have been even more painful for a moral person to face. So, in the case of "Elisabeth von R.", he slowly educed that she had been in love with her sister's husband. When she heard the dreadful news that her sister had died in childbirth, the thought flashed instantly into her mind (according to Freud's account) that now her brother-in-law was free and she could marry him. Unable to cope with this wicked thought, she repressed it by converting it into physical symptoms.

Freud is a beautiful writer, creating compelling, suspenseful narratives. He said that he couldn't help it if his case studies read like short stories.

In the year of this first book, which marks the beginning of psychoanalysis, his sixth and last child, Anna, was born. He dropped hints that his active sex life was over. He was barely 40, his wife 35. During the next five years he went through a period of dark, anguished self-searching. His father's death, in 1896, affected him deeply. He experienced lonely sadness, mixed with periods of euphoria; worried about real or imagined health problems and his children's short-lived but recurrent illnesses. Oddly superstitious for a man of science, Freud believed he would die of heart failure before he was 50. He set about a self-analysis, concentrating on his dreams. This process he shared with a close friend from Berlin, Dr Wilhelm Fliess, in revealing, emotionally intense letters not fully published till 1985.

He struggled with a sense of failure. Having convinced himself that hysterias had their ultimate origin in childhood incest – abuse by a father or other adult – he became troubled by believing that he had been wrong; that the disturbing hints he had seen in his own and his patients' dreams and memories had been a fantasy, dating from the fourth and fifth years of their lives; and that this fantasy was universal. The Oedipus complex was born, so called from the Greek myth, the subject of Sophocles' *Oedipus the King,* of the man who had involuntarily – as it were, unconsciously – killed his father and married his mother Jocasta.

There may have been a quasi-incestuous situation in Freud's own household. Martha's younger, unmarried sister, Minna, came to live with them and stayed indefinitely. A freer, more intellectually curious woman than Martha, she would sometimes be Freud's companion on holidays. Jung, Freud's disciple, then rival, would claim that Minna had confessed to him that she and Freud had had an affair. Most have dismissed his allegation as malicious; but in 2006 a diligent researcher discovered a registration, in Freud's hand, at an inn in the Swiss Alps: "Dr Sigm Freud u frau", short for "Dr Sigmund Freud and his wife". It is known that Minna was with him on that holiday in August 1898. Of course, he might have been economizing on one room. If not, a taboo love affair is another possible reason for his disturbed though highly creative state in those years.

In 1900 he published a lengthy work based on his dream analyses, *The Interpretation of Dreams.* His theory that dreams are disguised wish-fulfilments has been much questioned; but his magisterial account of the rich symbolism of dreams fully justifies the proud epigraph he took from Virgil's *Aeneid:* "Flectere si nequeo superos, Acheronta movebo" – "If I cannot bend the higher powers, I will stir the lower depths." Dreams were his path into the unconscious.

In Freud's view everything in the psyche has its origin, mostly sexual, in early childhood. He believed this with the zeal of a Messiah, and expected any disciple to follow the creed: in the beginning was infant sexuality. The memory of it would be repressed later, because it was too uncomfortable; but it was always there. In neurotics – and aren't we all, to some extent? – some element of the earliest stages, the oral, the anal and the phallic, covering our first three years, or the ensuing Oedipus complex, was still causing problems in adulthood.

Unfailingly honest, Freud adjusted and added to his theories over time, but never swerved from the sexual bedrock. In the years after his dream book, he was reviled for denying the innocence of childhood; but also began to attract followers. Vienna soon had a little group of psychoanalysts, with Wednesday evening discussions in Freud's waiting room over black coffee, cakes and cigars. They were all Jews at first, to Freud's regret; but then came a welcome breakthrough – the enthusiastic support of a Swiss psychiatrist, Dr Carl Jung, who came to visit him in March 1907. Jung was young, tall, robust, aggressively direct in manner – and a Gentile. Freud joyfully saw him as his spiritual son and heir. The movement would be safe in Jung's hands, after Freud's (self-predicted) early death.

Invited to give lectures in the USA, Freud, Jung and a lively Hungarian analyst, Ferenczi, made a successful visit there in 1909. From that point psychoanalysis had a bridgehead in the New World, and went on to flourish. However, against Freud's wish, the American Association would later insist that only physicians can become psychoanalysts.

Jung began to doubt that neurosis almost always had a sexual cause, and their close friendship turned sour. The movement split. The clever Alfred Adler had already gone – a strong socialist, sickly in his childhood, he believed that a drive for power, not sex, was the key to neurosis. In Freud's eyes this made him an apostate and beyond the pale. Freud could be a good hater. He said he needed someone to love and someone to hate, and often found them in the same person. He could also feel deep affection, as a multitude of warm, wise and witty letters reveals.

If the case study of "Elizabeth von R." had seemed, even to its author, to read like a short story, there are later studies which read like novellas – "Dora" and "The Wolf Man". They are again beautifully written, absorbing narratives, in which Freud is the Sherlock Holmes of the mind, ultimately solving his patients' intractable problems from minute clues. Modern critics claim he got both patients wrong. Even the real-life "Wolf Man" said in old age that he didn't really believe Freud's analysis of him had been correct, but Freud was a great man and knowing him had been the richest experience of his life.

Other important works from the early years of the century include *The Psychopathology of Everyday Life,* a study of "slips of the tongue" and oversights, and *Three Essays on the Theory of Sexuality.* Belatedly Freud was awarded a university professorship.

Vienna, home to Johann Strauss, Egon Schiele, Gustav Klimt, Arthur Schnitzler and Ludwig Wittgenstein, was at a pinnacle of cultural splendour, but also chaotic with political unrest – national enmities and anti-Semitism. Mahler conducted at the Opera – and the young, angry Hitler often listened and watched from the cheapest arena. The First World War brought Freud the anxiety of having his three sons in arms, fighting for the Central Powers; the eldest, Martin, became a prisoner of war. With the armistice in 1918, the long-decaying Austro-Hungarian Empire finally collapsed. In Vienna there was hunger and massive inflation. With no heating, Freud huddled in his overcoat while listening to his patients. He was better off than most, since he had some foreign patients who paid for each session with a ten-dollar bill.

Word came in 1920 that his beloved second daughter Sophie, married to a Hamburg photographer, had died in the great flu epidemic which was killing more than the war had done. Freud was desolate, but kept working. The death of Sophie's infant son, three years later, rendered him almost inconsolable.

Anna, his youngest child, was his remaining bright hope. He analyzed her, his own daughter, against all Freudian orthodoxy. She never married: how could one replace one's father *and* psychoanalyst?

The darkness of the times, as well as ageing and tiredness, must have contributed to Freud's strange, almost mystical work, *Beyond the Pleasure Principle*

(1920). Beside the primitive urge for pleasure – Eros – he now recognized a self-destructive impulse: Thanatos. In war victims and grieving children, he witnessed a compulsion to repeat painful experience. There was, he thought, some profoundly conservative impulse to return to an earlier phase of existence; and the earliest of all was non-existence. This is a philosophical explorer, a poet, writing.

Another short, darkly philosophical book, *Civilization and its Discontents,* appeared in 1930. In it he reflected on the impossible conflict between our individual desires and the restraint necessary to build society. There was no hope either from religion or Communism. Someone once told him that the Bolshevik Revolution in Russia would entail a period of chaos and destruction, followed by endless wellbeing. He replied, drily, that he half-believed this.

He was by now a cancer survivor. In 1923 his upper jaw and palette had had to be cut away, and he had been fitted with a hideously painful prosthesis. He could no longer talk or eat comfortably, but could still smoke his beloved cigars, even if sometimes it meant prising his jaws apart with a clothes peg. And he went back to work. He courageously endured further operations over the years.

In 1930 he was awarded the Goethe Prize for Literature. He had always valued, and quoted, Goethe and Shakespeare above any psychoanalyst. Three years later the Nazis burnt his "filthy" books, along with those of Thomas Mann, Einstein, Zola and Proust.

Following the *Anschluss,* Hitler's occupation of Austria in 1938, the Freuds were in extreme danger. When Anna was taken into Gestapo custody for a day, this made her father's mind up. President Roosevelt had ordered US embassy officials in Europe to help the Freuds, and a faithful Welsh disciple (later his first biographer), Ernest Jones, pulled high-level strings in Britain to get entry permits.

Obtaining exit permits was harder, but eventually, after extortion of money, the permits came, for almost the entire Freud family. His mother – formidably cantankerous and talking Yiddish to the end – had mercifully died at last, aged 95. One of Sigmund's sisters had gone to the USA, the other four decided to stay in Vienna: they, and Freud, did not think the Nazis would want to harm four quiet, elderly Jewish ladies.

The other Freuds, with trunks and suitcases, doctor, servant and their pet chow, went by train and ferry to England. Freud, always an Anglophile, was warmed by his reception: even strangers wrote wishing him well. After a short period renting, the family moved to a comfortable house in Maresfield Gardens, Hampstead, in north London. More of Vienna arrived, in the shape of furniture and other effects, and Martha, Minna and Anna bustled about, making a downstairs room seem almost a replica of the consulting room at 19 Berggasse. His innumerable classical and Egyptian statuettes, the embodiment of psychoanalysis burrowing into the past, were positioned around him exactly as before.

He was growing weaker, and in great pain, but still wrote. His last work, published early in 1939, was *Moses and Monotheism.* It propounded the idea that Moses, actually an Egyptian, had been murdered by the Jews he had led to freedom – a primal parricide, leading to eternal Jewish remorse and the search for a redeeming Messiah. Freud was an iconoclast to the end.

Bombs fell on London. This was civilization's compulsion to repeat, and its death wish, with a vengeance. "Will this be the last war?" his doctor asked. "Mine at least," said Freud. Later that month, in agony, he told the doctor that his life made no sense any more, and reminded him of a promise. The doctor administered a dose of morphine. Freud died on 23 September 1939.

He had changed our sense of ourselves, of what makes us what we are, more than anyone else in the 20th century.

The four old ladies, his sisters, died in Nazi death camps. Anna, a famous analyst herself, jealously preserved his memory and reputation until the end of her life in 1982.

NOW LET'S START TALKING...

Over the following pages, Sigmund Freud engages in an imaginary conversation covering twelve themes, responding freely to searching questions.

The questions are in italic type;

Freud's answers are in roman type.

ON HIS CHILDHOOD

Freud's parents were part of the great exodus of Jews from the eastern margins of the sprawling Austro-hungarian Empire fleeing persecution and poverty in the second half of the 19th century. Jacob Freud, a wool merchant, was 40 when sigmund was born in a small Moravian (Czech) town in 1856; his wife Amalie was twenty years younger. Jacob already had two grown sons – one with a wife and two infant children – from an earlier marriage. Sigmund's half-brothers soon emigrated to England, where they started businesses. The main Freud family headed for the imperial capital, settling in Vienna when sigmund was four.

Do you take your coffee black, Professor?

Thank you. But what I really want is ... Ah, blissful! Frankly, your promise of cigars is the only reason I came.

I wish I could have offered you a fee.

Money doesn't bring one happiness, because it's not a childhood wish.

Neither are cigars, nor my own weakness – cigarettes.

But masturbation is ... Now, what do you want to ask me?

Far too much for the time we have. But let's start with your early childhood.

A very good place to start.

If by some miracle I could visit your home in Freiberg, 150 years ago, to gaze at you in your cradle, what would I find?

Just one room. We were quite poor. You'd see a kindly-looking long-bearded man, aged about 40, and a plain woman a bit older, perhaps rocking the cradle. You'd think, Ah, his grandparents. You'd see my mother, a pretty girl gazing down adoringly at me, her young good-looking husband sprawled nearby. You might also see two other infants, obviously my little brother and sister. But you'd be wrong in all your guesses except in the case of my mother. The middle-aged figures are actually my father and Monika, my Czech nurse; the young "father" is my half-brother Philipp; and the two other infants are his older brother's children – so, bizarrely, my nephew and niece. This scenario assumes that Monika has brought them to our room too, so she can look after all of us infants together; and that Philipp has dropped by because he and my mother like each other. They're both young, you see.

An intriguing family group! In a sense you had two mothers, your real mother and your nurse.

A child can't have too many mothers.

What was your nurse like?

She would scold me for clumsiness and dirtiness. She was Catholic, and would take me to Church.

Your parents didn't mind?

No – father was liberal and easy-going. I'm not sure what he'd have said if he'd known that Monika preached at me about Heaven and Hell.

That reminds me, you once said sex is where the highest and lowest are closest together, and quoted Goethe: "From Heaven across the world to Hell."

That's true. St. Teresa in mystical ecstasy and Jack the Ripper are both making huge mental efforts to obtain satisfaction. As a matter of fact I think the saintly ugly Monika gave me my first sexual experience. Don't ask me what, I don't remember. I do remember her bathing me in red water – obviously after she'd used the water, during menstruation.

A strikingly colourful image!

And I remember another colourful image: picking yellow flowers, dandelions I suppose, in a sloping meadow with John and Pauline, my nephew and niece. I loved them both. Pauline had the best bunch, and we tore the flowers from her. She cried, and ran to a peasant woman, who gave her some bread. I recalled this when I went back to Freiberg in my adolescence, and fell for a girl wearing a yellow dress – Gisela. The infant memory evoked by Gisela's dress is what I call a "screen memory", part-revealing and part-concealing another emotional event. It's not hard to see "deflowering" in the memory; and any curving, sloping landscape is your mother's body.

Have you memories of her – your mother – from that time?

There's one. Monika left – I was very upset, worrying that Mama would leave me too. My mother told me later they'd sacked the woman for stealing and she'd been sent to prison. "Boxed in," Philipp said in my infant memory – I thought he meant Mama was in a box. My fear homed in on a wardrobe, so he threw it open to show me she wasn't there. More fright: where was she? But then she walked in, slim and beautiful.

That's a romantic phrase...

Not entirely. Slim was reassuring to me, because it meant she wasn't having a baby by Philipp, or Papa. I was very confused. A wardrobe symbolizes a woman's "insides" – I knew babies grew there. She'd given birth to Julius, who died after eight months. I'm sure I felt remorse over wishing him ill. And lately she'd produced a baby girl. I didn't want another one, taking her away from me! I saw her naked once. That was when we were leaving rustic peaceful Freiberg, my beloved early home, for Vienna. We shared a sleeping compartment. She must have undressed. *Matrem nudam,* I called it, for the benefit of the puritans – "mother naked". We men always see our mothers as we first saw them, don't you think? – slim, beautiful ... She adored me, of course.

What was your father like?

Gentle, kind, humorous. Like Mr Micawber in *David Copperfield* – not very dynamic at business. Passive, while Mama was strong. There are both sexes in us all – so *four* people are always present during intercourse. I only fully realized when Papa died how wise he was.

I think I'll have a cognac. Would you like one?

A glass of Marsala would be welcome.

ON THE ROOTS OF SEX

Early in his medical career, in 1884, Freud experimented with cocaine, and just missed becoming the discoverer of its use as a local anaesthetic for the eye. He would have to wait another twenty years for fame in the field of psychology. By now almost 50, he was the head of a bourgeois family, with six children to support; but his new science of psychoanalysis was anything but bourgeois. His *Three Essays on the Theory of Sexuality* (1905) brought a storm of indignation. There were a few supportive voices, including the respectable *British Medical Journal,* which in a two-page review praised the author's courage and tenacity in the pursuit of truth.

Let's move from your own childhood to your theories about childhood sexuality. They were enormously controversial – you were reviled.

Childhood was the age of innocence, you see. No matter how shamefully we behaved in later life, leave us our early innocence, we beg you!

I thought *mine was innocent. When an uncle told me "the facts of life" at fourteen, I was simply incredulous. Then, a few months later, I experienced the wonder of my first erection – while on a ship crossing the equator! – and the world was transformed. You're really telling me I was sexual from infancy?*

I really am. You were simply unconscious of it. You mustn't think of sexuality as confined to the genitals. Think of that first state: the greedy seeking out of the nipple, the gorging at it, and if the nipple isn't available, a thumb will do – or an ear-lobe or finger.

But isn't this just hunger?

It starts from hunger, the self-preserving grasp at the breast, but soon there's the discovery that touch, taste and smell bring excitability. Hence, the libido, the sexual instinctual drive. Who can see a baby as it sinks back from the nipple without being reminded of lovers, satisfied and sleepy after orgasm?

I've little experience of babies at the breast, and have an aversion to milk – but I can see the similarity.

I hope so – otherwise you'd have been better off talking to those more respectable gentlemen Adler and Jung!

I much prefer talking to you. You found there were three stages: oral, anal and phallic – could you explain those?

They correspond to the areas which successively bring auto-erotic pleasure to the infant. The mouth I've dealt with; then, during toilet training, pleasure – as well as sometimes pain – is found in the anus. Infants – who don't feel disgust – will often hold back the stools so as to increase the pleasure when they finally come. Next, the phallic stage – masturbation. All infants masturbate. Many a tired nurse has got her charge off to sleep by tickling the genitals.

Or worse ... so I've read.

Or worse. Many people carry remnants of those early stages into adulthood – even fixations on them. So, for instance, oral personalities may be passive and dependent, may smoke or drink heavily, and place an over-emphasis on kissing, including perverse kissing. If they're really disturbed, they may develop a disgust with food. Or, say, with milk!

By "perverse kissing" you mean oral sex?

Yes. I imply no moral judgment – I simply mean an act diverted away from normal intercourse. Well, then, the anal stage. A hangover from this can result in obstinacy, thrift, orderliness, prudishness. Nature made it difficult for us – but also intensely interesting – by making the organs of excretion virtually the same as the organs of sexual pleasure.

There's a powerful line by Yeats: "But Love has pitched his mansion in the place of excrement." ... Is there a phallic personality type?

Someone more interested in conquest than relationships.

In creating psychoanalysis, you worked on the theory that some early disturbance, lingering on as you've described, was responsible for your patients' problems. Is that correct?

It was more than a theory, I assure you. I found it again and again. Infant sexuality has elements of all the perversions – sado-masochism, homosexuality, voyeurism, exhibitionism, fetishism, and so on. In the adult, those elements constellate to give people their particular sexuality. But say sado-masochism lingers on, one can either repress it or give vent to it. Only decent, moral people develop hysterical neurosis: feeling an urge so disgusting to them that they bury it deep in their unconscious, whereupon bodily symptoms break out like boils. Bad, immoral people just do the deed! A neurotic is a criminal who is too cowardly to commit the crime.

You split the psyche into three components, the id, the ego and the superego. Could you explain those?

First of all, they should be the "it", the "I" and the "over-I", as in my German. I also never invented such phoney words as *parapraxis* and *cathexis* – I wanted people to understand I was writing about *me* and *them,* not some jargon-ridden medical textbook.

Couldn't you have controlled the English translation? "Ego" sounds cold, reminding us of egotism.

I know, it's a pity. But my daughter Anna approved the translation and I didn't want to upset her. The id – to use the term familiar to English speakers – is primitive, chaotic, dark, unaware of time and space, and with a pure aggressive lust for pleasure. The ego, born out of the id, is consciousness. It has to confront reality in a rational way, and is rightly scared of what the id is capable of. In infancy the ego is in a weak, unformed state: all it can do is repress, produce forgetfulness. The superego, which enters the ego gradually, is the imposer of rules. It's the strict father, and it makes us guilty. It is necessary – otherwise there would be anarchy, everyone doing what they want, no society or civilization. The trouble is, the strict fathers – and mothers – who impose the rules forget their own childhood, and are too harsh.

Talking of harsh fathers or mothers – the male child also has a fear that his penis will be cut off as a punishment, if I understand you correctly?

Yes, arriving at the phallic stage, which starts at around three years old. It's a universal fear, and is reflected in many myths. Kronos cut off the genitals of his father Uranus, for example. Some parents do actually say, "If you don't stop playing with yourself, I'll cut it off." this is a terrible threat. Even if it's not spoken, the fear is there. A young boy may catch sight of his sister, and think it's already happened to her. Little girls may see their brothers, and think it's already happened to themselves.

They envy them their penises...

Of course.

Did you never feel that individuals are too variable for a universal model to apply?

No. People vary but the basic structure is determined.

I haven't yet met a woman who will admit to penis envy – it makes them angry with you.

I can't help that.

Many will say they fear it, as an instrument of man's violence...

I didn't agree to see you to argue over penis envy. It's what I and many others, including female analysts, observed again and again. Let's move on – we haven't yet reached the most vital conflict of our early years.

I think I know the one you mean...

ON THE OEDIPUS COMPLEX

Freud first used the term "Oedipus complex" in 1910, but had made the breakthrough more than a decade earlier, during a period of depression, loneliness and uncertainty. At that critical time he had decided to try to analyze himself through his dreams. This led him to a decisive theoretical change: from believing that most hysterias involved early paternal seduction to becoming convinced that these were mostly fantasies; and that the fantasy was universal. He continued to add to the new theory – for example, by exploring the role of "Oedipus" in bisexuality and in women – over the next three decades, believing it to be the "nuclear complex" for all neuroses.

Once, travelling to Delphi, I passed the crossroads where Oedipus killed his father. It was a hot, still day, and I had a strange, surreal feeling, as if I was partly absent. I recalled someone saying that Oedipus has no unconscious because he is our unconscious.

I visited Athens in 1904; and I too had a very strange feeling when standing on the Acropolis. I suddenly wondered if it really existed. I managed later to pin down my unconscious thoughts there. In my youth I'd longed to see it, as part of a casting-off of the narrowness and poverty of my home; yet when I finally achieved it, I felt guilty at having gone beyond my father, who'd been too poor and uneducated to go there, or even want to ... I envy you seeing delphi, the site of the oracle, the *omphalos* of the ancient world.

Oedipus ... When does the complex begin, and what is it?

It normally happens in the fourth or fifth year of life. Like Oedipus, none of us can avoid his or her fate, which is to feel passion and jealousy toward those closest to us, overlaying and mixing with our turbulent infantile sex drive. There is a wish to create a child with the parent of the opposite sex. Of course, the infant is not aware of how this can be done. But the urge is there, powerfully; and there is also the desire to do away with the parent of the same sex, who stands in the way. Of course, because of bisexuality, the reverse can sometimes happen...

The complex should *be resolved quite early, am I right?*

Yes – when a boy confronts the horror of castration. That should usher in a long period when the sexual drive is latent – lasting until puberty, when the libido bursts in with fearsome power, as you described happening to you as you crossed the equator. With girls it's somewhat different, the complex fading much more gradually, and sometimes not at all.

You had your own Oedipus-style royal tragedy in Vienna, didn't you? Crown Prince Rudolf, a double suicide with his mistress after sex...

True. It almost killed his father, the Emperor – he may have intended that. Every suicide is also a murder. The Viennese breathed sex and death in those years.

Can you tell me how you discovered the complex?

It stole up on me during a bad time, in my late thirties, when I was quite poor and unsuccessful. I felt isolated and depressed. Out of this frozen state would sometimes come creativity and illumination. Also my father died, and I grieved intensely for him. I started to analyze my dreams. There were ambivalent dreams about my father. In one of them, around the time of his funeral, I was late arriving for the ceremony. I saw a notice, "You are requested to close the eyes." Well, of course a son must close his father's eyes after death – carry out his pious duties.

But also I felt it meant, please close your eyes to forgive how I felt about you. At the same time I brought to light my early erotic awareness of my mother, such as seeing her naked on that train to Vienna. All this, and what I was seeing in my hysterical patients, their seduction fantasies, worked unconsciously on me. But then one day I was on the point of giving an injection to one of my patients, an old lady, but realized just in time it was the wrong injection – it might have killed her. My almost fatal mistake had been caused by my mind straying. A male patient had related a dream which pointed to his having had intercourse with his mother, and I was thinking about that. As I left the old lady, my brain reeling from having almost done violence to her, the idea for the Oedipus complex flashed into my head. "no more concealment," as the old Greek dramatists used to say!

But when you say your patients had seduction fantasies, isn't it true that for a long time you believed they had been seduced by an adult?

That is true. For a while I believed a childhood seduction lay behind all neurosis. It was very painful having to abandon the idea – I was left floundering, with nothing to put in its place. Till the truth struck me.

What caused you to abandon the idea of parental seduction – we today would call it abuse?

Partly it was my own growing awareness of the importance of sexual fantasy in myself; and partly because the accusation of a seduction came from my patients so regularly that it strained credulity. Not all neurotics could have been seduced. I saw neurotic behaviour in my own brothers and sisters – well, and in me – and I absolutely couldn't believe my gentle, decent father had done any of that.

I have to tell you, in recent years a few critics have accused you of deception and dishonesty – they claim you changed your story out of cowardice, fearful of offending people even more. I've never believed that.

I'm so glad! I'm sure these people earned a lot of money by attacking me in such a monstrous way. Do they really think it was less offensive to my fellow men to learn they'd all wanted to fuck their mothers and murder their fathers? Forgive my coarseness. No, it was an agony, being forced by evidence to relinquish one theory for the other. I felt sick about it – I *fell* sick. I thought at any time I'd die of a heart attack.

I'm glad we've dealt with that. Actually, anyone who reads your correspondence with Wilhelm Fliess, your close friend from Berlin in those years, would see the agony you went through and...

How do you know about my correspondence with him?

It was published in full in 1985.

Oh my God! such a betrayal. I wanted those letters burnt. There was a bit of homosexuality lingering in my psyche, which made me pour out my heart to him.

The letters did you honour: they show you as human and vulnerable, tender to your children, worrying about their illnesses, proud of their little achievements and so on.

Well ... this has shaken me. Is nothing sacred and private?

I might as well ask you about a personal matter at this point. You had Minna Bernays, your sister-in-law, living in your house, helping your wife with the children...

Poor woman, her fiancé had died of tuberculosis – she had nowhere to go, and no financial means. I was close to her, she was strong-minded, very intelligent. She believed in my ideas, and became my closest confidante. What's all this about?

In an interview, Jung said you and she had had an affair.

Oh you don't want to take any notice of that scoundrel! I stand for an infinitely freer sexual life, but I myself have made very little use of such freedom – only so far as I considered myself entitled to.

Recently some sleuth found an inn in the Alps, where you'd signed for a room as "Dr Sigmund Freud and his wife"...

So? can't one sleep with one's wife anymore?

You were on holiday with Minna on the date in question, in August 1898. I don't think it matters whether you slept with her or not. You may even have felt "entitled to", if Martha had grown sick of frequent pregnancies. She may even have been complicit. Turning a blind eye. Who knows the secret arrangements of a man and wife?

Are we discussing Oedipus or hotel registers?

I apologize ... Before you had your flash of inspiration, had you been thinking of the Oedipus myth?

No. But of course I did so immediately after, and reread *Oedipus the King.* And then I realized Sophocles' tragedy is like a metaphor for psychoanalysis – the long obstinate resistance, and gradual opening-up to the blinding truth. The great authors knew everything, long before me. Incest is everywhere in mythology, and myths are like a tribal dream. The incest taboo, so powerful everywhere: how to explain it except that the urge is so strong?

Very true. You're not denying that actual abuse – seductions – take place?

Of course not. Just not nearly so often as fantasies about it.

Not long ago there was a massive witch hunt. Under hypnosis, and heavily prompted by psychotherapists with an agenda, women in droves claimed to have retrieved memories of childhood abuse. Their loving fathers were falsely accused, and often imprisoned, on the basis of these so-called retrieved memories alone. Lately, the whole thing has been discredited, hundreds of the accusers have recanted, and the therapists are being sued for millions. Vast damage has been done.

Akh, will humanity never learn? these so-called psychotherapists used my theory of repression yet denied the Oedipus complex.

Not merely denied – hated it. We have many such witch hunts.

So hysteria thrives.

ON THE TALKING CURE

Freud's consulting room, crammed with ancient artefacts, evoked a suitably timeless world, in which long-buried secrets could be unveiled. Between patients – always greeted with a handshake – he would pace around the separate living quarters, where family and servants moved quietly. The concept of psychoanalysis had its tentative beginnings in the 1880s. A kindly older physician, Joseph Breuer, knowing Freud was interested in "nervous" complaints, consulted him and shared patients. The predominance of sexual factors in the stories that emerged eventually scared Breuer off, but intrigued Freud. He managed to persuade Breuer to co-author *Studies in Hysteria* (1895), including the seminal case study of "Anna o.".

I'd like to ask you about the so-called talking cure. But first I must apologize again for my impertinence just now.

It was interesting. A slight aggressiveness, probably because the Oedipus complex had touched a nerve. You *wanted* me to have slept with my sister-in-law to match your own Oedipal desires.

I can't trace any jealousy toward my gentle father ... except I suppose I did split up my parents most nights by begging to be allowed into their bed. Mum would always go to my room, though I'd probably have preferred Dad to leave. I was afraid of ghosts, you see.

Ghosts can be very troubling – and there are so many.

So – the process of analysis, the talking cure. If I were your new patient, tell me what would happen. The famous couch – how did you decide to use that?

I couldn't stand being gazed at for so long. So I'd sit behind. I found that having patients lying down encouraged them to relax and let their minds wander. The whole effort of psychoanalysis is to get them to remember the past, so they can move on. Dreams were a great help, and if they were completely relaxed, all the better. I'd also ask them to close their eyes.

"You are requested to close the eyes."

Ah, you remembered my dream! Yes, that dream was also advising me to analyze my feelings toward my father. I'd let my patients wander where they willed, in free association – just going with the flow.

It reminds me of how a poem is made. The American poet Robert Frost said that a poem rides on its own melting, like ice on a hot stove.

Good analogy! Yes, the ice slowly melts and moves. The analyst should interfere very little – it's a bit like mountain-climbing for the patients: they feel their way up, then unexpectedly – through free association – find they are being led a different way, maybe sideways, to find a better path. I thought of myself as just a mountain-guide. The climb can take months, even years. You see, the patient doesn't want to be cured! of course she'd like to be free of the terrible symptoms, but they've been created for a purpose, to block off dreadful knowledge and guilt. I learned that hysterical symptoms represented their sexuality: a nervous cough, for instance, might have taken the place of a fantasy or memory relating to fellatio. It's vital to unblock the repression, but the patient creates defences and deceits to avoid doing so. How painful it was for Elisabeth von R., whom I wrote about in *Studies in Hysteria,* to acknowledge that she'd been in love with her brother-in-law, and was therefore glad her beloved sister had died in childbirth! an amoral, wicked girl wouldn't have been tormented.

You published that book with Joseph Breuer...

Yes. He was older, already established as a physician. He would send patients to me or consult me, out of generosity partly. Also he had cases that dumbfounded him. We used hypnosis in those early days. I was a complete greenhorn, still in my twenties, just engaged, and fumbling in the dark.

What would you say was his main contribution to the new science?

Well, he contributed a lot. If I'm honest, it's almost impossible to disentangle his early ideas from my own, because we discussed our cases endlessly. He knew he was dealing with repression, but he could only use hypnosis to dig behind it. Ultimately he became rather frightened – by eros.

His most famous case was that of "Anna O.", Bertha Pappenheim – later a famous social worker and feminist.

Yes, she was a bright girl from a prominent Orthodox Jewish family. Her symptoms were extraordinary. And kept changing. Hallucinations of skulls, of her fingers turning into snakes, a paralyzed arm, chronic cough, tiredness, inability to drink water, headaches, visual disturbances, speaking in tongues – several languages mixed up. You name it, she had it. Breuer spent thousands of hours at her bedside. He found all her symptoms were related to her father, who had just died. Being rather prim, he did not think sex played any part in her illness – even though, in the end, Bertha went into a phantom pregnancy, with Breuer the seducer, and he had to flee in terror, taking his jealous wife off to Venice for a second honeymoon!

What did you learn from her case?

That apparently nonsensical symptoms could have a meaning. As Breuer managed, more by luck than judgment, to trace a particular symptom back to an unpleasant event in her past, the symptom disappeared. Though usually another would then take its place. Even though she herself coined the phrase "talking cure", Breuer exaggerated his success with her. Well, in the end he ran away from her!

Some say her hysteria was her only escape from the boredom of a restricted life, and had little to do with sex.

Oh, she was writhing around in a phantom pregnancy, bearing Breuer's child ... yet her problems had little to do with sex? Very likely!

Tell me about transference.

That was at first a curse. I found that, encouraged to free-associate without censorship, patients were projecting on to the analyst feelings they had had for a central early figure – usually their father or mother. They would be aggressive or compliant, fearful or competitive, and so on. There might be a strong erotic attachment, as happened with Bertha. Later I realized I could use this, as a tool for understanding, and for making them see that the emotions tormenting them belonged to the past, not the present. Women often saw their mother in me, alas.

And what about counter-transference?

We're only human! We can find ourselves responding inappropriately to the transference. That's why later I insisted all analysts should be analyzed themselves. It's another reason I sat behind them: some women would arrange their skirts rather carelessly ... Well, that's enough for today. Unless ... those ghosts of yours ... I could perhaps help...

That would be a great honour. I'd like to tell you about a dream from about 30 years ago I've never forgotten.

Then why don't you switch off that damned recording machine?

ON DREAMS

One of Freud's richest works, the fruit of his long self-analysis, is *The Interpretation of Dreams* (1900). Slow to be widely noticed, it sold 351 copies in the first six years. Dreams, Freud theorized, were attempts to fulfil wishes that were deeply repressed in our unconscious. Often these were shameful, resulting in distortions "censoring" the material. We have to become code-breakers, aware that the dream might mean the opposite of its surface meaning. Whether or not one accepts his theory, the book is an immensely daring journey into the psyche's underworld – at the beginning of a century which would bring to reality nightmares of violence on a massive scale.

Good morning, my friend! I trust you slept well ... oh, this is so kind ... a box of Don Pedros! How did you know these were my favourite cigars?

I looked up "Freud" and "cigars" on ... well, it wasn't hard to find out.

Thank you. I've been thinking about that mid-life dream you told me. Let me see if I can summarize it ... You were listening to a piano recital in a cathedral. The pianist, a young woman, was lumpy in build, and hammered the keys atrociously. At the interval, a bishop announced she was the illegitimate daughter of the poet S.T. Eliot and a shopgirl, born in Canterbury. He said her name was "Orchard", not "Lees". Whereupon, slim and attractive, she started playing with dazzling lightness, and you felt joy and relief. Do I remember it correctly?

Eliot was T.S., not S.T. But I like your version, because it's "toilets" spelled backwards.

Ha! A Freudian slip – he once heavily criticized my book, *The Future of an Illusion.* now ... Dreams are wish-fulfilments. Sleep relaxes the censorship, so repressed wishes emerge from the depths. But the relaxation is not total, so a compromise is reached, part revealing, part concealing. Your dream plucked two unimportant names from your memory: a miss Lees, a lumpish student of yours, and Ida Orchard, a soprano who sang at village concerts with your mother and father.

Audrey *Orchard. I'm amazed by the dream's poetic skill.*

Even cleverer is the way "Orchard" not only completes a powerful symbol of regeneration – "lees" means the dregs of wine – but also brings in your mother, whom miss Orchard represents, being pretty and a fellow soprano. This is a common feature of dreams – condensation. With great economy the dream will create a composite figure or image. Miss Lees-Orchard represents your mother, who first showed you that cathedral, and also your mistress at the time of the dream. Penis/pianist is a delightful pun – and I'm sure she could play with exquisite lightness on your keys ... But you said she could be cold to you because she hated being "the other woman". You sometimes thought just the lees of the affair were left.

A dream is over-determined: each element covers multiple factors in your life. The recital concerns your sexual life, but you were a performer in another sphere, too, a poet – alluded to by the Eliot reference. You needed a regeneration in both aspects of life.

Dreaming that a great poet had an illegitimate child encouraged me to take risks in my writing and not worry about giving offence – I'm aware of that now.

So, a wonderful dream! Mother, mistress and yourself turning from dregs to fields of fruit! Your mother's gnarled hands become the soft, pliant fingers which first excited your infant skin. Your awkward mistress realizes how lucky she is to have a poet for her lover, even if he's married! *You* are re-energized in bed and on paper. No wonder the dream made you happy.

There's one association I haven't told you. Eliot wrote a play called murder in the Cathedral, *about the killing of Thomas Becket, the saint, in Canterbury cathedral.*

I did know that, and that it was first produced in your birth year, 1935. I, too, have ways of checking things out, my friend. It's not surprising you should have had a death wish against your humble, saintly mother. She was old, lonely and crippled, you felt guilty at rarely seeing her ... Dreams enjoy ambivalence, they like expressing contrary ideas in the same image. Eliot sanctions your oedipal wish, but also, through his play, your death wish. In dreams it's never either-or, it's and-and. However, from your happiness at the end I'd say Eros won the day – or rather night.

What about the reductionist idea that most dreams are just nonsensical, jumbled-up re-runs of recent events?

No, dreams use recent incidents or the day's residue to help create the psychic drama. By the displacement onto seemingly trivial material, the unconscious evades the censor.

Like writers in a totalitarian state.

Yes, that's true. I once dreamed I was in company at table d'hôte, where a woman put her hand on my knee intimately, but I removed it. She said, "oh, but you have such beautiful eyes." Now, the night before the dream I had been having dinner with friends, and one, an oculist, allowed me to share his taxi home. I made some joke about the taxi meter starting as soon as you get in, and it was like a restaurant where the bill rises fast and you're worried it will cost you too much. Idiots could say I dreamed about table d'hôte and eyes because I'd been with an oculist and had mentioned restaurant bills. But my unconscious had just *used* these. If I went into all the associations, I could show the dream was about love and what it costs. Often too much! The meter starts whirring. Perhaps I didn't want to move the hand from my knee. Some elements of the dream are too personal to talk about, even now.

That's sad ... Couldn't you be a little more forthcoming?

If I tell you she was my sister-in-law, whom I had to support, you will think it confirms infidelity, but you should not rush to conclusions. Anyway, it illustrates displacement: the real dream-thought may be only a fragment of the manifest dream.

Are all *dreams wish-fulfilments? Surely there are anxiety dreams?*

Naturally, if the wish is shameful and taboo-breaking, it will create anxiety. But I'm a little tired...

The Interpretation of Dreams *is a great book. You had to go so deeply into yourself.*

I remain rather proud of it.

ON THE WOLF MAN

A rich, depressed and obsessional young Russian aristocrat, who had been in and out of psychiatric hospitals, became Freud's patient in 1910. The analysis continued for many years. Freud published his account, *From the History of an Infantile Neurosis,* in 1918. The patient became universally known as the "Wolf Man", from a childhood dream which Freud interpreted in a highly imaginative, many would say fantastic, way. The Wolf Man went on to be treated by some of Freud's followers, and survived into advanced old age. If Freud had helped him, as it seems he did, it may have been because the patient found in him a kindly father-figure.

Your most famous dream interpretation was that of Sergei Pankeyev – the "Wolf Man". You analyzed him for four years before World War I, and for a few months after...

When I did it free of charge. He came from a very wealthy Russian Christian family, but his money vanished with the Revolution. I felt sorry for him.

Yet I've heard his first words to you were, "You Jewish scoundrel, I'd like to fuck you from behind and shit on your head!" Is that true?

Something like that, but he was really a pleasant, decent man, with terrible problems – obsessional neurosis, depression ... he fell in and out of love in a lightning flash. That greeting helped me, like a criminal's fingerprints. You analyze it, Dr Watson! You've read the case study: what do you see already?

Well, I can see homosexuality, of course...

Which he repressed all his life.

Anal-sadistic urges – he adored taking servant-girls from behind, especially if they had large buttocks.

Very good. He wanted to demean women because his highly intellectual sister had naughtily seduced him when he was about three, playing with his penis.

Let's come to his famous dream – when he was four – which ever after haunted him. Could you summarize it?

His cot was near a window. It was winter. The window swung open, and he saw several wolves sitting on the branches of a tree, white and motionless and with pricked ears, staring intently at him. Terrified, he woke up screaming. His nurse rushed to calm him. But the image was so lifelike it was ages before he could accept it was only a dream. What struck him most was the wolves' stillness and their strained, intense gaze.

He even drew it for you. Five wolves. And from that dream – working with him for years – you traced its origin to something he witnessed as a one-year-old, which was...?

His parents copulating while thinking him asleep. Part of the time at least *more ferarum,* like animals. He could see their genitals. His mother had no widdler – it had to have been cut off! that would only occur to him later in infancy, after his nurse scolded him for masturbating, and threatened to cut *his* off if he did it again. In the dream, the violent motion of intercourse has been deflected into stillness; the opening window, his awaking eyes; the wolves, father-substitutes.

And the whiteness?

Underclothes, bed-sheets.

It's a startling leap, from the dream to what you say evoked it. And in the case study you even seem to admit you can't quite explain what led you to it. Did your interpretation come more from intuition than science?

No. I admit it seems incredible. And I do give an alternative, that he might have seen animals copulating and imagined his parents doing it. But once we stumbled on the primal scene, as I call it, every puzzle made sense. For instance, it explained why, when the little child came upon a servant-girl kneeling to scrub a floor, he showed excitement by weeing himself. He imagined his mother – and then himself – in her position. The seduction by his sister made him passive; he developed an inverted Oedipus complex; he wanted a baby by his adored father. But for that to happen, he would have to suffer castration. In fear, he repressed his homosexuality. You could say it withdrew into his bowel: he could only defecate with the aid of enemas. What was left for his adult life was an anal-sadistic, and masochistic, attitude to women.

Did the discovery of the primal scene have a good therapeutic effect?

Oh yes. Everything opened up then for us, and he improved greatly. That too convinced me I was right.

He was interviewed, in his eighties, by a Viennese journalist. Apparently he told her he didn't believe in your analysis. He was still struggling with girlfriend problems when he died, aged 92.

Ha! Not bad at 92! I'd call it successful, given how sick he was, and that his sister and father had committed suicide. But I expect patients to be ungrateful.

The Wolf Man did say you were a great man, a genius. And his dream, and your interpretation of it, continue to fascinate readers, after almost a century. It wouldn't do so unless the two images, wolves in a tree and the primal scene, connected for us at some deep, mythic level.

To see your own father put part of his body into your mother, then as it were attack her violently, is quite powerful. I myself witnessed this, I believe. When I was about eight I dreamed I saw my mother laid on her bed by two men who had bird beaks, and I was terrified she was dead, because of the serene look on her face. I think that years earlier, drawn by a strange noise, little Sigi must have stumbled into his parents' bedroom just as they finished. It's not for nothing that orgasm is referred to as "the little death".

"Bird beaks" suggest Egyptian gods, who fascinated you.

Yes – and "to bird", *vögeln,* is an obscene German verb, like "to fuck". I'd just been told that, at the time of my dream, by a *concierge*'s son – called Philipp.

Like your half-brother. Do you think the two men in your dream were your father and Philipp?

It's possible.

Do you think your own experience of the primal scene affected your analysis of the Wolf Man's dream?

Absolutely not.

ON ART AND LITERATURE

Steeped in classical and modern European literature and art, Freud drew from and wrote illuminatingly about such great artists as Sophocles, Leonardo da Vinci, Michelangelo, Shakespeare, Goethe and Dostoyevsky. His paper *The Moses of Michelangelo* (1914) reflects on the statue with intensity, perceptiveness and modesty. His long study of the German novelist Wilhelm Jensen's story *Gradiva* (1906) and his analysis of Leonardo da Vinci (1910) are beautifully written works of art in themselves. It is not surprising that nowadays literary scholars appear to value Freud more than psychoanalysts do. John Dryden's description of poets "moving the sleeping images of things towards the light" could apply equally to Freud.

You also wrote a case study of Leonardo da Vinci...

Yes I did, that was a *jeu d'esprit* – partly a novella, if you like. He had difficulty finishing works. I wondered if I could find a psychological reason for that.

It's an ingenious, beautiful work. One is tempted to say, if it's not true, it ought to be! Can you, again, outline the novella's plot, so to speak.

Leonardo recorded in his notebook a childhood memory, or rather fantasy – he wrote "it seemed to me...," suggesting it was a fantasy. A vulture flew to his cradle, opened his mouth with its tail and struck his inner lips several times with it. I recalled that the vulture was the ancient Egyptian hieroglyph for the vulture-headed goddess Mut, and also for "mother". The tail in his mouth surely represented the mother's breast – and also the phallus, at a time when he still thought his mother had a penis like he did. So, let's look at the great artist's mother ... Well, he had two.

Just like you, in a sense. "One can't have too many mothers," you said. Is that because you can split the bad from the good?

That was a joke, my friend. Leonardo was illegitimate, and it's quite possible he was raised alone for a time by his actual mother, a peasant-girl. She would have lavished all her lonely love on him, aroused him erotically and turned him toward homosexuality.

If I can interrupt, you believed a male homosexual has had an over-tender mother. In later life he puts himself in his mother's place and seeks a male he can love as his mother loved him. Am I right?

It's one of the ways it can happen. Of course, it may be constitutional too. Anyway, Leonardo's father married a woman of good class, and they took the child into their house. Isn't this why, in his painting of the Virgin and Child with Saint Anne, in the Louvre, Mary and her traditional mother look the same age? and have the same enigmatic smile, since Leonardo had by then met the mysterious Mona Lisa, who awakened his unconscious memory of his peasant mother?

A fascination with enigmatic lips!

Yes, reserved yet seductive ... Such was my speculation. And after the work appeared, my colleagues started to find vulture-shapes all over the painting. Jung even found one in Mary's pubic region.

But in fact Leonardo wrote "kite", not "vulture". You'd read a bad translation. Does that invalidate your theory?

Not altogether. I still think the bird's tail was the mother's breast. I'm even grateful for the mistake – otherwise I'd never have written the study. And I still believe it likely that his real mother's overtenderness paralyzed his will, froze him into a largely asexual life – and made it difficult for him to complete his paintings. His repressed sexuality turned into a lust for knowledge and invention. He sublimated.

We haven't mentioned sublimation. What is it?

When the impossible desires of childhood come up against brute reality, some people can use those instinctual energies in nobler ways, helping to create civilization and culture. So, if a musical youth had a perversion about women farting, he might learn to play the trumpet!

Ah, but if he simply repressed it in his unconscious, he'd become neurotic and maybe develop terrible haemorrhoids!

Oh, far worse. It's what I did – sublimate, I mean – becoming a scientist. Yet sometimes I wished I had had poetic talent. I admire artists and writers greatly, and envy them.

Why is that?

Because they seem to evade the normal rule that you have to give up the pleasure principle. The artist is like a child playing with his own fantasies, and in doing so he turns them into a new kind of reality. He seems to have a faulty censorship, giving him a ready opening into his unconscious. He doesn't have to deny eros. He can indulge himself sexually because Eros is the source of his art, don't you think?

Renoir said he painted with his prick...

It must have been very busy!

There's a book called Blake & Freud *in which the author Diana Hume George argues that you resemble the English Romantic poet William Blake in your call for a liberated Eros. She says you were essentially a poet, only you weren't aware of it. I agree with her.*

That's flattering, but - if you'll forgive me - shit.

Let me try to persuade you. You both go into dream and myth - the unconscious. Symbolism and metaphor are vital to you. As in poetry a single word or phrase can carry several meanings; opposites can fuse in the same line or sentence. Think of Hamlet's lustful abuse of his mother, "The rank sweat of an enseamèd bed..."

Ah yes, desire and revulsion...

Also I suspect you relied a lot on intuition. You wrote to Fliess that you found a way out of a block "by renouncing all conscious mental activity so as to grope blindly among my riddles". That's just like a poet working: he may get a little drunk, stop thinking logically, then go into a kind of dream-writing.

Ah, I never got drunk ... I was a humble worker in Solomon's mines, I couldn't carve the stones for Sheba's jewels. Psychoanalysis is simply the *science* of the unconscious. I do agree that we can all touch poetry, at least of a surreal kind. For instance, that worthy gentleman who wrote inviting his estranged American wife to sail on the *Lusitania* to join him in Europe, so they could try again. A ship that had been sunk in the war! He meant *Mauritania,* but his ship

– his slip – showed his true feelings. His unconscious took over for a split second, and transformed him briefly into a wit, a surrealist, an Oscar Wilde!

And into the wife-murderer Crippen! I remember it in your Psychopathology of Everyday Life *... Shall we pause there? I've another dream I'd like to tell you.*

Good. But first, bring on the cancan girls. If I'm really a poet as you say, I'd better start behaving like one.

ON CARL JUNG

Carl Jung (1875–1961) was a highly influential figure in 20th-century thought. In his early thirties he became an enthusiastic and warmly welcomed follower of Freud, and was for some years his chosen successor (there were nineteen years between them in age). Then a rift opened. Unlike Freud, who knew only of neurotics, Jung had long experience of treating psychotic patients in a Swiss clinic, and could not accept that the root of mental illness was almost always sexual. Freud could change his own mind, and often did so with great honesty, but could not be tolerant of his disciples' "heresies". Jung went on to give as much importance to spirituality and religion as to science.

I can tell, from the occurrence of the Jungfrau in the dream you've just told me about, and the snake you saw in the grass, you're going to ask me about Jung. Well, I don't want to talk about him.

Not even briefly? He caused you to faint, didn't he, just before you, he and Sándor Ferenczi sailed for a lecture tour in America in 1909? Why was that?

He was talking about peat-bog corpses dug up in Germany. I saw he had a death wish against me. I fainted again in his presence in Munich in 1912, after we'd fallen out but were attempting to be reconciled.

Is it true that when you recovered from that faint you murmured, "How sweet it must be to die"?

No.

Thank you for clearing that up. Can you tell me your first impressions of him, when he visited you in 1907?

We talked for thirteen hours. I was very struck by him. I liked the word-association tests he'd developed at his clinic. The emotional response that certain words evoked from patients was fully in line with free association. He thought my *Interpretation of Dreams* a masterpiece, which of course was flattering.

Physically what was he like?

Very imposing. Broad-shouldered, clean-shaven, very tall – more soldier than scientist. Bullet-headed, close-cropped. Gold-rimmed glasses. A Siegfried. And giving off great energy. I was completely taken in.

And very quickly you saw him as your natural successor?

Yes. Though I should have seen problems ahead. For me it was tremendously important that he was not a Jew. He was, and looked, every inch a Germanic Aryan. My small band of followers was almost entirely Jewish – it would have encouraged anti-Semitism. I was willing to tolerate some extension of the libido, beyond sex, as he wanted, for the sake of having my Christian Saviour. Well, he turned out to be my judas.

You were friends for four years before you discovered that?

More than friends, a kind of father-son bond. But after a while his letters became cooler, more disputatious. And when he published a paper called *Transformations and Symbols of the Libido,* my dream crashed around my ears. He proclaimed the libido was some vague, mushy "psychic energy", much broader than I or psychoanalysis could tolerate.

It sounds as if he was rebelling against the father.

Well, of course. Deeply neurotic.

And the final straw was a rendezvous that he missed?

Oh yes! I was going to Lake Constance to visit a young Swiss colleague who was facing a serious operation. I forewarned Jung, expecting him to come the short distance from his home to meet me. He never turned up. Later he told me a farrago of contradictory lies – my letter arrived late, he'd been away that weekend, he expected me to visit *him.* I could see then we were well rid of him. Why did I ever believe in that pseudo-mystical charlatan?

Was there nothing he wrote later that you admired...? Alright, we'll move on.

ON "DORA"

Freud's *Fragment of an Analysis of a Case of Hysteria* (1905), better known as "Dora", continues to arouse controversy. It is his only long case study of a woman. The background situation, a tangle of seduction, hypocrisy and deceit in two bourgeois families, might have been a fitting theme for the contemporaneous Viennese author Arthur Schnitzler – whom Freud saw as his literary "double". Critics re-analyzing "Dora", aided by the exquisite lucidity of Freud's account, accuse him of being blind to the obvious: that the depressed and neurotic young woman was a victim of patriarchy and bourgeois hypocrisy. Perhaps the truth lies somewhere between Freud's interpretation and that of his critics.

Will you talk about the girl who ran away, the patient you called "Dora". Ida Bauer was her real name. The Bauers were near neighbours of yours, weren't they?

Yes. We knew them quite well. Philipp Bauer was Jewish, charming, cultured, rich, and riddled with syphilis. Katie, his wife, suffered from painful gonorrhea, presumably a gift from her husband, and expressed her anger by obsessional cleanliness. Locked rooms, windows wide open in winter. Not surprisingly, family life was equally locked and frigid. The son, Otto, conscience-stricken at seeing his father's overworked, malnourished Bohemian millworkers, embraced Socialism. And then there was Ida, bright, engaging, cigarette-smoking, who loved her brother and father and couldn't stand her mother.

Understandably. Bauer brought Ida to see you, aged eighteen, suffering from depression and hysterical symptoms...

A chronic cough, breathlessness, loss of voice, migraine ... I learned about her family's friendship with another Jewish couple, the Zellenkas. For many years, Bauer and Frau Zellenka had been carrying on much more than a friendship.

A man with advanced syphilis? Wasn't he impotent?

I imagine they had oral sex – certainly Ida's nervous cough showed she believed so. Ida was terribly upset by her father's affair; yet spent a lot of time at the Zellenkas, mothering their children, and sometimes sharing a bedroom with Frau Zellenka, who had, she said, an adorable white body. They seem to have talked about everything, including sex. So there was the complication of an adolescent crush on a woman she ought to have hated as a home-wrecker!

And what about Herr *Zellenka? How did he react to his wife's affair?*

We know he had a fling with a governess. Then when Ida was fourteen he tried to kiss her passionately. She told me she'd been disgusted and run off; but I couldn't believe she had no sexual response. She must have felt his erect member pressed against her.

Must have?

She said she felt pressure on her chest. An obvious displacement. A couple of years later, when they were walking alone by a lake, he propositioned her seriously. Even though they'd exchanged long letters, and she'd accepted flowers from him every day for a year, she slapped his face and ran off. One reason may have been hurt pride – the governess had recently told her about his little adventure with *her.* Ida told her mother, who told her father, who confronted Zellenka. He claimed Ida was obsessed by sex and had created a fantasy. Bauer believed him, or pretended to. In Ida's view, he didn't care what happened to her as long as he felt free to carry on his affair in peace.

He was pimping his daughter, in effect?

Let's say it would have been convenient for him if Zellenka were distracted. I was convinced she loved him, but repressed it by reverting to her Oedipal desire for her father. This emerged from a dream about a house on fire and a jewel-case – no need to tell you what *that* means – which linked her father and her would-be lover, who had given her such a case. Her dream was effectively saying, Dear Papa, save my precious jewel-case from the fire of temptation ... I felt the case, the analytical case, was opening up to me with wonderful ease. Her *"No!"* to some suggestions had such emphasis it was clear she was saying yes.

For you, when did a "no" actually mean no?

Oh, one learns to read the signs. For instance, while denying that she had ever masturbated, Ida kept putting her finger in the open purse on her lap. Her actions spoke louder than her words!

Do you think, in questioning her about sex so intimately, you were – to use a modern phrase – "turning yourself on"? Exciting yourself?

I always made sure I used dry medical terms. To come back – I suggested to her she wished Zellenka to ask his wife for a divorce, so he could marry her. And indeed that could have solved a lot of problems. Then she announced she would give me two more weeks – if she wasn't cured by then she was finishing. I saw, too late, Ida had developed a strong transference to me; desired and resented me; and by quitting so abruptly was avenging herself against both her father and Zellenka.

But she was cutting off her nose to spite her face!

Well, she was terrified of having her fantasy turn into reality, like all neurotics. I felt very angry – I couldn't afford to lose a patient. She also broke off with the Zellenkas, and did it very sadistically: when one of the Zellenka children died, she combined a condolence visit with telling Frau Zellenka she knew of her long affair with her father, and made Herr Z. confess to his wife that he'd lied about Ida and slandered her.

Vengeance is Ida's!

Do you know what she went on to do with her life? She became a professional bridge player! Still the subtle deceptions and negotiations; still the foursome! She married, not very happily. But the bridge-playing – what a sublimation!

I should tell you your "Dora" case study has become a rod for critics, especially feminists, to lash you with. They say it's outrageous that a young girl should not have been believed when she told you she felt disgusted by his embrace.

My observation of Ida told me her response would have been far from simple revulsion.

They also say, here was a girl caught up in a sordid situation, regarded as inferior both as a female and as a Jew. They say her hysteria arose from patriarchy and a family at war, a mother who was unloving and a father who exploited her.

Every age is convinced it alone knows the truth. I didn't allow enough for the transference, but I would stand by my interpretation. She did clearly love Zellenka.

Did you perhaps show some antagonism, envying Zellenka having someone young and vivacious like her? I noticed, when we were discussing my dream, you mistakenly said Ida instead of Audrey.

Ah, so you wish to analyze *me!* ... Well, there may have been some counter-transference. Dora means gift in Greek; she gifted me her jewel-box; and I did wonder, after, if I should have shown her more affection.

You once, rather surprisingly, said psychoanalysis is a cure through love.

It's true. I should have shown more of it to Ida ... But at least her depression lifted.

The more thoughtful critics acknowledge that you helped her, when no other doctor had been able to.

I'm sure I did. Other doctors dealt with hysteria with tubes in the rectum, electric shocks and hot rods to the spine. But enough ... let's talk privately again. Last time your ghost was about to make an appearance...

ON WOMEN

Strangely tentative about the female psyche, not until 1933, in old age, did Freud attempt a theoretical survey through a lecture, "On Femininity". He hardly registers mothers as ongoing child-rearers. His love for Martha, his wife, may have contained some resentment that her comparatively poor family had added to his burdens. While liberal in supporting easier divorce, abortion and homosexual rights, he held conservative views about the nature and role of women. Most feminists are hostile to his theories, though he has some warm defenders. Of his concept of a woman's "penis envy", Jung remarked that the penis is only a phallic symbol – that is, of man's power: an interpretation that may make it more acceptable in modern times.

Martha put the toothpaste on your toothbrush every morning. You believed woman's place was in the home?

I trained accomplished female analysts, and treated them with equality. Find another profession where that happened! But in general I thought women were happiest looking after a home and children, and the best chance of their avoiding neurosis was sexual intercourse within marriage. But for many women, that wasn't possible. Their marriages amortized. I felt enormously sorry for them: their husbands could freely take mistresses or go with prostitutes.

So what should such women do?

Have an extramarital affair. Far better that than develop hysteria. As I told you before, I was in favour of a much freer sexual life.

How would you have felt if Martha had had an affair, when your own sexual life had cooled?

I would have been amazed she had the time or energy left over from bossing us all to keep the house clean!

She was like your "Dora"'s mother?

Not to that extent, thank God. I have to say, though, that I was often struck by a sort of psychic rigidity that overcomes women in their thirties – as if there's little scope for further development. I speak of women in my time, of course. Perhaps *your* women have become lifelong psychic dynamos! But not ours, on the whole – it was as if the effort to become women at all had exhausted them.

Why, is it harder to become a woman than a man?

Yes. A girl has additional changes to go through. Both sexes have the same love object at first: the mother. But a girl's changes. She realizes that she does not have a penis; neither does her mama, so it must be her fault. The infant girl resents her, even as she starts to want to make a baby for her papa. Her antagonism to her mother may continue for a long time, possibly all her life; though she will feel guilty and try to over-compensate. Often she will look for a husband who resembles her father. As often as not, she will later replace the husband with her first son! Another change which a boy is spared is the discovery of a new sexual organ, the vagina. So, becoming a woman can be exhausting. Some never succeed.

In your lecture "On Femininity", you described women as narcissistic, more jealous and envious then men, less capable of sublimation and inventiveness – except for plaiting and weaving – and with little sense of justice. Did you always try to flatter women like that?

Ah, but I made it clear that male and female doesn't precisely equate with masculine and feminine: we're bisexual. The learned women in that audience were quite narcissistic enough to know I didn't mean *them!*

You would be lynched by feminists if you said that now.

Women may not like it, but I didn't create Nature! Through his different anatomy and development, the male's superego, his "over-I", is stronger. His Oedipus complex comes crashing down when fear of castration assails him. Taking his father's place with his mama would mean punishment, the *chop* – so, no thank you! This shock leads to the creation of a severe superego. In contrast a girl has no Oedipus complex until she discovers her lack of a penis and starts to want a baby by her father. She doesn't fear castration, because it's already happened, so to speak. So she can linger in the complex, without the motivation to develop a strong superego. That means less sense of justice and cultural creation. And her penis envy leads to narcissism and jealousy. However, there are plenty of narcissistic, jealous men, and women who are without a trace of vanity or envy, and highly ethical.

What about a man's envy of the vagina? I would love to be a woman for, say, a month.

For a month would be interesting, I agree. But you didn't, in infancy, feel wounded by not having a vagina. The vagina doesn't exist in the unconscious, because neither sex is aware of it till puberty. A few women told me they were aware of it, but they were probably confusing it with the anus. My friend Lou Salomé believed that even in mature women the vagina is only on lease from the anus. A clever metaphor!

Don't males suffer breast envy? And the womb – I had a friend whose anus bled whenever his wife had her period.

There's a narcissistic wound when the breast is withdrawn. But most men don't envy women their breasts. Of course, unjustifiable legal and social restrictions do also affect women's natures. And if society tells women they mustn't think about sex, they can lose interest in any sort of thinking.

The women you knew had no sense of your belittling them?

No! I treated men and women the same. I had strong friendships with many. Lou. Minna of course...

The American poet H.D., a patient and friend of yours, wrote a loving tribute to you; and her partner Bryher said you were like an old-fashioned family doctor who would go out in all weathers and at night to help someone.

That was kind of them. Hilda – H.D. – was a splendid woman. When she was in analysis with Havelock Ellis, and found he was fixated on watching women urinate, Hilda obliged him. Now that's tenderness. Women can be very generous.

But you believed they could also be dangerous, I think?

I thought that they could hold a man back. For achievement, a platonic homosexual relationship may be best.

Is the libido, the sexual drive, the same in men and women?

It's the same. But I fancy it becomes more restrained in a female. Nature needs more libidinousness in the male for the propagation of the species. Frigidity can be a problem in women. Certainly not in Lou, who told me, on one of our late-night walks, she wanted orgasm *constantly!* So women *can* be more sexually voracious than men, being closer to Nature, more hostile to culture.

So, sometimes voracious, sometimes frigid ... Would you say you had to struggle to understand women, just as a woman struggles to achieve her femininity?

That's true, I did. I called woman "the dark continent". I couldn't decide what they really want.

You don't write much about maternal nurturing – simple mother-love. Why is that?

It wasn't my focus. I left it to others.

Which is the true Freud: the one who seems to suggest a woman is a wounded, incomplete male; or the one who wrote of the overriding power of the three women – the mother who bears one, the beloved chosen in her image, and then Mother Earth? You said, "It is in vain that an old man yearns for the love of woman as he had it first from his mother; the third of the Fates alone, the silent Goddess of Death, will take him into her arms."

Woman is the guardian of eternal Eros. Perhaps I only fully realized this when man's stronger superego produced the cult of the *Führer.* I must also say it was the Jewish women who stood up to the Nazis most courageously in Vienna – my beloved Anna not least ... Now please switch off again, I'd like to hear more about this man who menstruated.

ON BEING JEWISH

Thoroughly assimilated though he was, rejecting Jewish religion and rituals, Freud never lost a strong sense of being Jewish. His house-guests were almost invariably Jewish. When he was struggling for recognition at the University of Vienna, he was able to lecture on his ideas to his Jewish social and cultural society, B'nai B'rith ("Sons of the Covenant"). As anti-Semitism gathered force in the lead-up to World War II, he became more sympathetic to Zionism, wishing for Jews a place of freedom, but wishing too it could be somewhere other than in Palestine. His long-living mother continued to speak Yiddish, and her influence on him remains enigmatic: one author, Estelle Roith, has called this relationship "the riddle of Freud".

When he was a young man, in Galicia, a Cossack pulled off your father's Sabbath cap and threw it in the gutter; and your father just meekly picked it up. When he told you about this, it upset you, am I right?
Very much. I lost a lot of respect for him.

Was your father ashamed of what he'd done?

Not enough! You have to understand the Jewish mentality in those primitive *shtetls.* brain was valued over brawn. The most respected men were scholars, palefaced, short-sighted, with long beards and a stoop from poring over religious books. These were the men the girls sighed over! it was the wives who did the physical work. My father, in accepting abuse from a Cossack, would have been seen as behaving with admirable self-restraint. But that's not how I saw it.

You, as a brilliant boy, were growing up in German-Austrian culture, in an emancipated home. It must have been quite hard for your father and other Jews to adjust to a different concept of manhood?

It *was* hard for them. The Gentiles, with their athletic prowess and Prussian-style militarism, despised Jewish males for their effeminacy. Self-hating Jews felt the same: Otto Weininger, the philosopher, shot himself – in Beethoven's house! – because he felt Jewish men were no more than women.

What did being Jewish mean to you?

A shared, ancient ethical strength. Of course, there was also anxiety. We middle-class Jews had achieved almost complete emancipation. Yet then, as we filled up the law schools, medical schools and newspaper offices, because we're intelligent and ambitious, the anti-Semites grew more and more vociferous.

You spoke and wrote perfect German, and you knew Hebrew?

Yes, I was taught by a brilliant professor.

Yet in one letter you denied even knowing the Hebrew alphabet.

Did I? I must have had some good reason for pretending. But I had cast off all the religious stuff. And we all feared the *Ostjuden,* the caftaned hordes streaming in from the East, because we knew their arrival would increase hatred toward all Jews.

Did the Bible play a part in your life, as a boy?

My father owned a Philippson Bible, which was rather revolutionary in its time. It was in Hebrew with a German translation. It discussed archaeology and comparative religion. And, despite the injunction against graven images, it contained hundreds of woodcuts showing life in Egypt. Papa let me read it when I was little. That's how I became fascinated by Egypt and archaeology, and identified with Joseph, interpreter of dreams. Papa gave me a copy on my 35th birthday, inscribing in Hebrew a message saying the spirit of god had moved in me when I was seven.

So he was *religious?*

Only vaguely – he'd given it up really. In his later years, though, he would pore over the Talmud, the rabbinic discussions of our laws and ethics.

I'm told its sentences are very antithetical, so can be read either positively or negatively. Not unlike the id's ambivalence...

Or the Delphic oracle's ... only a Jew could have created psychoanalysis. As a racial outcast I could think unconventionally. An atheistic Jew at that – an outcast from the outcast.

Let's come back to sex – I'm never loath to do that. Jews, I believe, have a robust, unromantic view of sex. No troubadours, no Heloïse and Abelard.

"Be fruitful and multiply". Just get married first, my son!

Has that influenced you? Your writings on sex seem more to do with tension relief than attaining ecstatic happiness.

I don't know that state! Where can I apply for an entry permit? Jews know it's important to have controlled sex, so that it can be got out of the way and one's main attention be given to intellect and the spirit.

Your mother ... you hardly speak of her, the years of your nurturing are almost as silent as those of Jesus. You did say that the mother-son bond was "the most perfect, the most free from ambivalence of all human relationships". That's rather idealistic and ... well, unambivalent for you?

I don't think it's far from the truth. A Jewish woman's romantic marriage is with her son.

She would have been shut out of the male Jew's world of learning, and on top of that she suffered from penis envy ... We know about the traditional smothering Jewish mama. Your father I assume, meek and mild, withdrew into the corner with his Talmud. Some have imagined your mother shouting and screaming, and torturing and frightening you with too much love – giving you some childhood trauma which made it impossible for you to...

Enough already! she was a wonderful mother. I know some of my children have described her as coarse, shrill, aggressive and selfish. But the word matricide never occurs in my works. Doesn't that say it all?

It could hardly be clearer. You must have been relieved she died before Hitler took over Austria.

Very. At last! I'd thought she was immortal, and therefore *I* wouldn't feel able to die. At 95 she hated a new photograph, saying it made her look a hundred!

It must have been very painful for you to leave Vienna?

Yes, even though I'd always said I hated the city. Eighty years is a long time. Anna said to me, "Papa, why don't we kill ourselves?" Hundreds of Jews were jumping out of windows – just as in your dream of young men crashing aeroplanes into skyscrapers...

That wasn't a dream: it really happened, in 2001. I said it seemed like a terrible dream.

It really happened? I must have been nodding off from the wine. My God, humanity is no better ... Anyway, I replied, "why make it easy for the Nazis?" And so we got out, and the English were very welcoming.

Your last work was Moses and Monotheism*...*

That's what *you* think! You know I wanted to write about the paranormal.

You mean...?

No, I'm joking. *Moses* was my last. That was no joke for the Jews. I wasn't sure it should be published when Jews were being so persecuted.

They were offended that you believed Moses was an Egyptian.

And that the Jews killed him, after he'd led them through the desert. A ritual sacrifice. The murdered father. I was speculating. Originally I was going to call it "a historical novel" – perhaps I should have done. It wasn't in any way meant to be offensive.

"Old men should be explorers," our friend S.T. Eliot wrote.

Ha!

ON DEATH WISHES AND HAPPINESS

In *Beyond the Pleasure Principle* (1920) Freud added a further instinctual drive, the Death Instinct. It was a drive that went beyond the id's urge for pleasure – the pleasure principle – to aggression against others and oneself. The larger problems of civilization, following the carnage of the First World War, increasingly absorbed him: the seemingly hopeless conflict between what we wish for as individuals and the need for order and restraint. God was an illusory father figure, religion a false consolation for our having to curb our destructive sexual and aggressive impulses. He thought – not surprisingly amid Fascism and Bolshevism – that most people were not lovable, but he remained personally kind and genial.

This must be our last meeting. That's sad.

For me too. I've enjoyed analyzing you briefly.

It's been a great privilege. When that dreadful event happened in New York I had a yearning to be able to ask you about it. There seemed no one alive – a century after your interpretation of dreams – *capable of deep psychology, of interpreting it in any but a superficial political way.*

I would probably only have been able to point you to *Beyond the Pleasure Principle,* in which I wrote about aggression and the death impulse. I was for a long time unsure about it, and many other analysts rejected it. They could accept my addition of an aggressive drive, for we had plenty of evidence of that already. But a *death* impulse they found hard to take.

I don't fully understand it myself. Can you help me?

The living organism seeks pleasure, or the relief of unpleasure. But I observed in my patients, and also in victims of war neuroses, an urge to remember and repeat very painful experiences. My mind went back to that unimaginable moment when inorganic matter first became organic. That would have created a tension the changed being would want to cancel out, by returning to the inorganic state. The same perhaps happened when consciousness first developed. So there may be a drive, beyond that for pleasure, to return to an earlier state – ultimately to inanimate life. "'Tis a consummation devoutly to be wished: to die...," as

Hamlet put it. I called this compulsion Thanatos, the death instinct, perpetually at war with Eros, the life instinct. The destructive young men you spoke of were obeying their death instincts.

They believed they were martyrs who would soon be enjoying all the delights of paradise.

They'll grow tired of those delights within a month! Life on Earth wasn't good enough for them – people find the ordinary pleasures and tensions of a peaceful life very hard to bear. That's the main reason for war.

Tell me about happiness.

Happiness has to be fought for against heavy odds, even if we've avoided poverty, hunger and disease. We are driven by our instincts, which demand to be satisfied, and which punish us, sometimes cruelly, if they are not. Yet they cannot, must not, be wholly satisfied; because if they were, there would be no family, no society, no culture and civilization. It's an insoluble dilemma.

You said the aim of psychoanalysis was to help people to be able to love and to work. You tried to make people happier by allowing them the freedom to be themselves, sexually – so you must have had some hope?

One had to try to change things. Morality has to become less harsh, because simply too much of what we yearn for is repressed. The cost is too great. But it's a balance. A little more freedom, a little less of the censor, is highly desirable.

Today's sexual morality, in the West, has become much more liberal.

Well, I hope the social cost is not too great. My fear was always that if sexual *mores* changed sufficiently to do any real good it would have unpredictable effects – because consciousness itself would change.

What, essentially, is psychoanalysis?

"Know thyself," the words carved on the Delphic shrine. If we know ourselves better, we can perhaps help others to know themselves and be a little happier.

Let's drink to that ... Were you happy?

I could love and work. And cigars never failed! But now I really must give up. The last draw ... so good!

But couldn't the compulsion to repeat include living again?

Who knows? I can't know everything, my friend.

NOTES

D.H. George, *Blake & Freud.*

"No individual can keep these laws..." W. Blake, *Jerusalem* 31:11–12.

"not at all a scientist..." Freud-Fliess Letters, J. Masson (ed.), 1Feb.1900.

"I can hardly contain myself..." *Letters of Sigmund Freud,* E.L. Freud (ed.), 16Jan.1884.

"Oedipus has no unconscious..." J. Starobinsky, quoted in D. Anzieu, *Freud's Self-Analysis.*

"I stand for an infinitely..." *Letters,* E.L. Freud (ed.), 8 July 1915.

The "cathedral" dream was first described in the author's memoir *Memories & Hallucinations* (London: Gollancz, 1988).

"by renouncing all..." Freud-Fliess Letters, 11 March 1900.

"a loving tribute..." H.D., *Tribute to Freud* (Manchester: Carcanet Press, 1970/85).

"It is in vain..." *The Complete Works of Freud,* ed. J. Strachey, Vol.12, p.301.

"the most perfect..." Ibid., Vol.22.

"Old men should be explorers" T.S. Eliot, "East Coker", verse 5.

FURTHER RESEARCH

WORKS AND LETTERS

Freud, S., *The Standard Edition of the Complete Psychological Works of Sigmund Freud,* J. Strachey (ed.), 24 vols. (London: Hogarth/Institute of Psychoanalysis, 1953–74)

Freud, S., *The Pelican Freud Library,* A. Richards, J. Strachey, A. Tyson (ed.), 15vols. (Harmondsworth: Penguin 1973–86)

Freud, S., ed. by **A. Freud,** *The Essentials of Psychoanalysis* (London: Hogarth, 1986)

Freud, E.L. (ed.), *Letters of Sigmund Freud* (New York: Basic Books; London: Hogarth, 1960/1)

Masson, J. (ed.), *Complete Letters of Sigmund Freud to Wilhelm Fliess* (Cambridge, Mass. And London: Harvard U.P., 1985)

McGuire, W. (ed.), *The Freud/Jung Letters* (London: Hogarth Press; New Jersey: Princeton U.P., 1974)

BIOGRAPHY

Clark, R.W., *Freud: the Man and the Cause* (London: Jonathan Cape; New York: Random House, 1980)

Gay, P., *Freud: A Life for Our Time* (New York: Norton; London: Dent, 1988)

CRITICAL STUDIES

Anzieu, D., *Freud's Self-Analysis* (London: Hogarth/Institute of Psychoanalysis, 1986)

Appignanesi, L. and **Forrester, J., Freud's Women** (London: Weidenfeld; New York: Basic Books, 1992)

Bettelheim, B., *Freud & Man's Soul* (London: Chatto & Windus; New York: Alfred A. Knopf, 1983)

Decker, H.S., *Freud, Dora, and Vienna 1900* (New York and Oxford: Macmillan, 1991)

George, D.H., *Blake & Freud* (New York and London: Cornell U.P., 1980)

Roith, E., *The Riddle of Freud* (London and New York: Tavistock Publications, 1987)

Storr, A., *Freud: A Very Short Introduction* (Oxford and New York: Oxford U.P., 1989)

ONLINE EXHIBITION

Freud: Conflict & Culture. Library of Congress.

www.loc.gov/exhibits/freud

MUSEUMS

Freud Museum, 20 Maresfield Gardens, London NW3 5SX. www.freud.org.uk

Freud Museum, Berggasse 19, A-1090, Vienna.

www.freud-museum.at

Made in United States
North Haven, CT
05 November 2026

21764037R00059